Wisdom

Andrew Zuckerman

Love

PQ Blackwell in association with
Abrams, New York

Wisdom

Andrew Zuckerman

Edited by Alex Vlack

Love

The heart is what matters most of all.

Kris Kristofferson

Nelson Mandela

A good head and a good heart are always a formidable combination.

Andrew Wyeth

Believe in yourself and believe in love. Love something. We've got to learn to love something deeply.

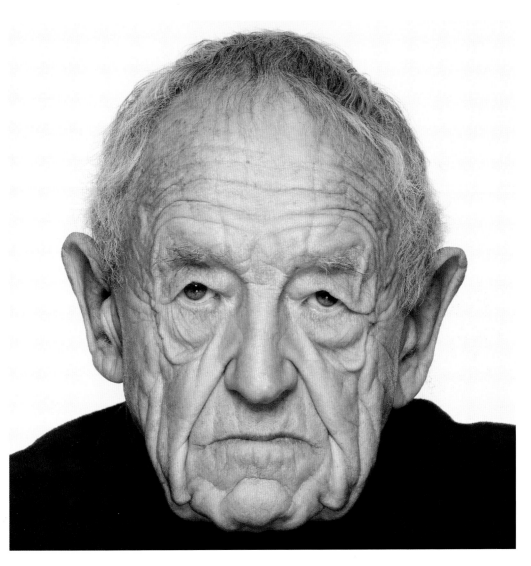

I'm married to a very strong woman of intelligence. She's been a great backer of my work. I remember when we first were married, we were having a difficult time being both young, married, and trying to paint; and she felt that it was difficult. I got word that the *Saturday Evening Post* was interested in getting me to do something for them, so I did this painting, just purely out of my imagination, looking down through a buttonwood tree. And I showed it to my father and he said, "Well, that'll certainly be difficult for them to understand. But they may like it. What are you going to ask for it?" I said, "A thousand dollars." He said, "You'll never get it." So I took it up to the editor-in-chief and I put it on the floor next to his desk, and he went and got some of his other people and they looked at it. And he said, "What do you want for this picture?" I said, "A thousand dollars." And he reached back and crumples up a paper behind him sitting on his desk, and I thought quickly, "Uh-oh." But I said, "That's just the rights of reproduction, the picture belongs to me." I went home. My father was thrilled that I had sold this picture for a thousand dollars. And my wife said, "That's wonderful." The phone rang, it was the editor-in-chief. He said, "We all love your painting and we want to commission you to do ten covers a year for the *Saturday Evening Post*." And Betsy looked at me and she said, "If you accept that, I'm leaving for good. You'll never be a painter." That was it. I turned it down. The picture is now owned by the Toledo Museum. And I found later he had been to the Museum of Modern Art and seen a show, Magic Realists—he thought it would be six or seven thousand dollars. That one phone call absolutely could've wrecked me. It's just that it didn't fit, and Betsy knew this about me. I remember the day I had all the Helga paintings that I had done, and I put them up in our mill gallery, up above, and there were two hundred and fifty drawings and paintings there, and I said, "Now, Betsy." I told her that I had done these pictures, which shocked the hell out of her. And before she went upstairs, she said, "These better be good."

You have to have freedom. An artist has to have that. My wife and I have had a very happy life. But it's been, I know, tough for my Betsy, because I need utter freedom in what I paint. And when I did that series of Helga, she knew nothing about it. They all said that she knew about it. She never knew a thing about it, because I was carrying on my regular painting, but I wanted to break loose, and I knew that she would be upset that I got this lady, who was married and had children, a German lady, to take her clothes off, and pose in every position I wanted. Utter freedom. I felt that my wife was beginning to track me, too much like my father did, and I just had to break loose.

Marriage is a terrific thing and I think there's certain ethical things you have to do, but if it starts to control you too much, watch out.

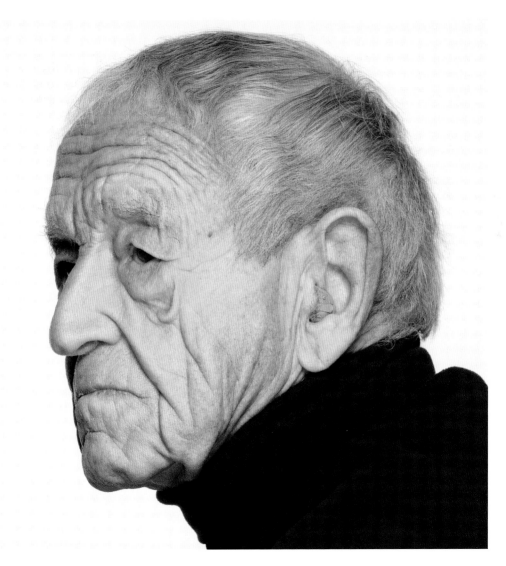

Jeanne Moreau

As long as I still adore and love what I have to do, I feel safe.

Give more expect to

than you
receive.

I don't know what makes a relationship work. Marriage is not for me. A relationship, it's generosity. Usually, people talk about love but they talk about passion, the attraction of the bodies and the passion in the first month and all that. And we know it doesn't work. Anyway, to stay sober on the subject, you give more than you expect to receive.

To be a free spirit is provocative. I tell you, I have no money and I don't give a damn. And with the financial crisis, people who were very rich lost the most. I didn't lose much. You see what I mean? As long as I still adore and love what I have to do, I feel safe.

Billy Connolly

Find what you should be doing and do it.

I keep returning to stand-up because that's what I do. And also because I spend all my money. I'm not in the millions class in the movies, so I couldn't live off that, anyway. But stand-up comedy is what I do. A one-man show is my living. It's what I was born to do. It's what I gratefully accept that I do. I'm very proud of it. I don't think I'm a film star. I don't see myself as an actor. I'm a comedian who acts, from time to time. I love doing it, and I try to do it very well, but the one-man show—the comedy stand-up thing—is what I do. I'm a very lucky guy. I was born to do it. There's a thing in Buddhism that says, "Find what you should be doing and do it," and it baffles a lot of people. I try to tell my children, "Just try and see what you're drawn to—the type of store window that you're drawn to." Like music stores, antique stores, tailoring stores—whatever it is you keep being drawn to. Because it's no mistake when you're drawn. Something's telling you, "This is the direction you should be going." It might be pet shops, it might be funeral parlors. Just try and notice what you're drawn to all the time. Because that's the way your life should go. And when you do something that you feel vocationally drawn to, it's not like a job. It's what you should be doing. It's your *raison d'etre*. It's the reason to wake, and you wake up feeling good in the morning, which is a wonderful thing. When I was a welder, an awful lot of the guys I knew didn't like being a welder. They didn't like their wives. They didn't like where they lived. And I thought, "God, imagine that's your life!" I found it quite frightening, the thought of going through life not liking your wife and not liking where you lived and not liking what you did. How do you wake up in the morning, going, "Oh God, here we go again?" You'd be on your deathbed saying, "At last! The day I've looked forward to all my life!" wouldn't you? I don't want to say that. I want to say, "Oh Jesus Christ, is this the time already?" When you're lying in your deathbed, say, "Is that it?"

I've no idea what makes marriage work, because everything's against it. What makes my marriage work is—I've no idea. Complete and total bafflement as to how the other person operates—that's what makes mine work. I'm very interested in my wife. I don't know what she wants to do. She likes to dive. And she likes being a shrink. And she likes to write. She likes to write serious papers. I don't know what she wants to do, you know? What makes my marriage work is that she makes it work. She buys the house. I don't know how you buy a car. She buys the cars. I don't know how you do anything. I've been looked after all my life by agents and managers. But she knows how you do stuff—she can book a flight on the computer. I don't know how you do that. I wouldn't know what to type in. Aeroplane? See if anything happens? My marriage works because she works at it, and I get the good attendance medal. I just show up. I let her call all the shots and I follow merrily. I do female things, like cook and wash the dishes and all that. And she does that traditional male thing of paying the bills on a Friday and all that. We have kind of swapped roles. Well, we haven't swapped roles, because we never had the other roles.

Sex is a good idea as well, from time to time. I don't have affairs. I lust in my heart, like Jimmy Carter. I like the idea of having sex with strangers, but I don't do it. But I think the idea is wonderful. And I'm very boring sexually. I'm not adventurous sexually. I think that would have killed my marriage, because I'd have to have thought about it. I'd have to come up with ideas. And I'm not very good on that front. I treat it pretty much as the last household chore of the day. And I think its plainness has helped me, as life has rolled merrily forward. I'm glad I'm not exotic, because I want so little from it—and I get it. She will kill me!

Sex is a good idea as well, from time to time.

Denis Healey

I've got a happy marriage, which is the most important singular thing.

Desmond Tutu

The secret to a successful relationship is knowing who is the boss!

No, it's actually all the obvious things that you are told, because it is so very easy when you are living together to begin to take one another for granted. We were told early on in our marriage—and we read things, too—that said it was the simple things, the courtesy of "Please, can you?" and "Thank you." You try to keep the romance going in your marriage, and so little gifts, remembering anniversaries; and the courtesies, trying to be the gentleman, opening doors, and offering seats, that kind of thing. And hopefully you share the most important things of your life, the same ideals, the passion for freedom and justice. People sometimes think I am radical in my political stance. I'm nowhere near as radical as my wife. She can get very, very, very hot under the collar about injustices. And it's also knowing that we still, all of us, like to be loved, want to be affirmed; and so telling each other about your achievements, the good things, "That's a nice meal," and, "Oh, that's a lovely dress," and, "Oh, you spoke well," or, "You preached well." It's quite amazing how you actually do need affirmation. You blossom when you have that and you wilt when it disappears. I have been very, very, very richly blessed. One time, the apartheid government was attacking me, and one of their cabinet ministers said, "Bishop Tutu talks too much." And I asked my wife, "Would you want me to keep quiet?" She said, "I'd much rather see you happy on Robben Island"—the maximum-security prison—"than unhappy outside because you kept quiet." And I've never forgotten the affirmation, the strengthening that I received from her and I give thanks to God for her.

When you are sitting in a traffic jam, you are usually fuming and angry and upset and frustrated, and probably annoyed with a few of the drivers behaving very badly. Imagine if instead of wasting all of that energy negatively like that, we tried a more positive way: imagine yourself as an oasis of peace, and imagine there's ripples that move away from that center of peace and touch others. If there were more centers of that kind of calm and peace we would be surprised, because you'd discover that instead of your blood pressure rising as it usually does in a traffic jam, you'd breathe more deeply, more slowly, and you'd begin to have good thoughts. My grandson used to say, "Are you thinking good thoughts?" If he'd done something wrong and he was wondering whether he was going to get a slap, he'd say, "Granddad, are you thinking good thoughts?" He doesn't know just how close he was in fact to the truth. In thinking good thoughts, we begin to affect our attitudes, in a very real way. We affect our health as well, because the calmer you are, the better it is for your metabolism. When you begin to lose your temper, the body begins to get ready either for running away or for fighting, and so the metabolism changes, and you have things moving away from your stomach and rushing into your bloodstream, getting ready for running away or for fighting. In thinking good thoughts, the opposite happens: a placidity over-comes you. Generally most of us, when you are not rushed, when you are not frustrated, do tend to make better judgments than when you are rushed and upset.

Serve

others.

God's dream is that you and I and all of us one day will wake up and realize an obvious truth, that each one of us is a member of the same family, the human family, God's family. A family in which there are no outsiders. All, all are insiders: Bin Laden, George Bush, Palestinian, Israeli, you name it. All of those we would wish to be on the outside, to exclude, in this family all belong. And if we were to realize that truth, we'd then say how could we possibly spend as we do, obscene amounts of money, on budgets of death, when a small fraction of those budgets we know would ensure that people everywhere, our brothers and sisters, had clean water to drink, enough food to eat. One day God thinks—God says, "I hope my children will wake up and realize that they are brother and sister." As Martin Luther King said, "If we don't learn to live together as brothers and sisters, we will perish together as fools."

For me happiness is when I'm able to make other people happy. Because it almost always is the fruit, the results, of not concentrating on me. If I say, "I'm going to be happy!" then I certainly know I'm not going to be. It is when I look away from me and am caring about the other that you will find happiness, and happiness is when you are serene, peaceful.

Serve others. The unfailing recipe for happiness and success is to want the good of others.

To be compassionate is to feel somebody else's pain, to recognize and feel somebody else's situation. We pay a lot of lip service to that idea, and it's easy to say, "Yeah, I know exactly where you're coming from."

I think rarely do people actually feel what's going on in another person. That's what real compassion is.

Rupert Neudeck

There is something in the hearts of the people, and in my heart, which is tangible, which cannot be communicated across great distances.

From the Bible, we have this wonderful story of someone who was hurt, who had been attacked on the way from Jericho to Jerusalem. And there were people going by, who were seen as "competent" people for relief and for support and assistance, and they were not touching this man. Only the one who did not seem capable of helping him was able to help. We are always able to do something, and we are always able to be touched. This is compassion. This is sympathy. This is something you can't deny in yourself.

In my life, in my activities, I was becoming aware of the very ambiguous position of prudence and intelligence—especially of academic and professional intelligence. Expertise; experts; knowledge. If we always follow academic knowledge and professional knowledge, we will never arrive at the idea of going into the sea to save people. There are many arguments against it, many very good arguments: it's too risky; the sea law jurisdiction is not defined; we are going into an area controlled by the Vietnamese Navy; we have to go into an area where there are pirates. It's dangerous. All arguments are against this activity. But then there is the question of whether you will do it. This is quite another question. That has nothing to do with experts. It has nothing to do with so-called "competent" people.

I was always aware of this: don't ask the experts. My government asked me whether I had asked the "competent" organization for what I wanted to do. Thirty years ago, I didn't know that there was an organization, but there was one. Everywhere in the world we have "competent" organizations. In Geneva, there was a United Nations High Commissioner for Refugees, and I went there. This man was "competent" for my request. And after I attacked him, when I wrote, "Are you doing anything? You have the competence as a world organization under the umbrella of the United Nations. What are you doing there?" he told me, "No, this is very, very difficult. We haven't yet taken up this case, and we can't go beyond the border to the other side to interview the refugees. How should we do it, interview people on the sea? We cannot put a table there!" That was before I knew that non-governmental activities go straight to the problems of people in distress, rather than to the "competent" people.

I never felt fear. It was always full confidence that we were doing something very good and that we, in a way, were protected. I never felt in danger myself. As a journalist, you see all these people in a much worse situation than yourself. Me, I can escape. I always have my ticket, my return ticket. They have to stay there. So that absorbs all fear. I always felt myself in a privileged position as someone with white skin with a good passport. I was always in a better situation. My government will pull me out of there in case something goes wrong. They have the obligation, and they will do it. But besides that, I always felt protected because I believed in it.

We are always able to do something, and we are always able to be touched. This is compassion. This is sympathy. This is something you can't deny in yourself.

When I was five years old, I went with my mother to sail on a big white ship. And an uncle of mine came to my mother, shouting loudly, "Why are you late, one hour late?" We missed the ship. And then we heard that this ship was torpedoed by three torpedoes by the Red Navy in the Baltic Sea, and more than nine thousand people were dying, drowning. So because we were one hour late, we had survived. I'm here with you in this interview because I was one hour too late. So this feeling came to me when I was in the South China Sea—that I had to do something where people were drowning in the sea. Because I was myself almost in the same situation, but I had been saved. And we Germans, we're all safe. And no one in the world has to care for us, because we did the war. We did the Holocaust. We did all this. There is no justification, no reasonable justification, for that. So now we have to give. Our country is now in a privileged situation, with our society, our Constitution, our economy. Now we have to give back. It's an obligation, a good obligation, an obligation which makes you happy, not something that is forced.

I can't think of an activity I've had to do alone. You have to live bonded to others. When my wife and I got married and when we had our first child, we were not aware of the work I was about to do. It happened suddenly. But we felt that the humanitarian work supported our life as a couple. Women, in a society like ours, feel underestimated when they only take care of their children and don't keep their jobs. And my wife decided to leave her job for the children when they were growing up. But then we were in this position where she could do the same full-time job inside our organization, and she could do it with the children, who were always with us. I always thought of that as a model for a normal society like ours, that people can do a lot being together when they are pushing together, putting all their energies together synergistically toward work.

Massimo and Lella Vignelli

Collaboration is sharing a philosophical platform.

M

There are many interpretations of the notion of collaboration. My interpretation, or our interpretation, is that collaboration doesn't mean both of us holding the same pencil, fighting each other, this way, that way, this way. Collaboration is sharing a philosophical platform. We have something in common. And to have elective affinities. That makes us understand a problem and provide the proper diagnosis so that we can work together. Then, who's working on it is irrelevant to a certain extent, because we fuse. But, at the same time, while we have fusion, we also have a diversity. Lella is much more practical than I am, so she can point out my weakness on that practical side. And I push in the other direction sometimes, so there is that continuous flow going from one side to the other.

L

Naturally, you have your own opinion. Your own opinions, many times, are very good. I balance the dreams of Massimo—always flying high—with what is reality. Sometimes I have to take him down a bit. The thing that was good for us is that we met when we were very young, and we've been together, and so we grow together in our interests, in what we like, and what we don't like, and what we discuss… judgment of design that we see, or architecture. We end up having the same interests. So the fact of growing together, through life, your intellectual capability is really what they call collaboration. The fact that you think the same way, or very close to the same way.

L

When we do a project, we work by subtraction. We come out, perhaps, with one or two ideas, and then start criticizing our ideas. But always giving a reason for the criticizing. Then we come to the heart of the problem and we feel that what we've answered filled the need.

M

Our process of working is really symbiotic in a sense. First we look for the semantic roots of whatever we do, and then we look for a consistency throughout, called a syntactical aspect.

L

Yes, exactly.

M

And then the pragmatic aspect—where she comes in—to see if everything works. Because if it doesn't work, if it's not understood, you might as well forget it. This is why design is different from art. Design has to be understood. It is a utilitarian profession. Art is not utilitarian. That's why design is. We always function for a utilitarian purpose. It takes a tremendous amount of courage to do things that have no utilitarian destination, and have the same kind of intensity, intention. And that is fascinating. Somehow, sometimes, the two things could be related, design and art. But what is never going to be the same is that one is utilitarian and one is not.

M

Between the idea and the execution, the idea is first. This is the greatest thing about ideas: either they come right away or forget it. It's terrific, that moment where you are interpreting the problem, whatever it is, and you come up with a solution. But, of course, it's your interpretation of a reality that counts; there's no reality, in a sense. It's your interpretation of the reality. Even objectivity, which has always been our research, is a very subjective interpretation. So we live with these nice contradictions within ourselves.

Dick Bruna

I draw every day.
Seven days a week.
I always go to my atelier.
I like that very much.

I've always done that. It's important to make your art every day. I always work on my own. I don't even talk about my work. My wife doesn't even know what I'm doing. I work sometimes for a month, and when it's finished, she's the first one who sees it. I show it to her, and she is a very good critic. I see it in her face. It is just like taking an exam or something. Her face reveals a "yes" or a "no." If it's a "no," I think, "I have to keep working on that." I need a very good critic, because when you're working alone every day, you don't see your mistakes.

When I was a parent, I was very, very busy with all those book covers, and I was a very bad father. I just saw my children in the evening, just before they went to bed, because I was just working hard every day. Nowadays, now that I am a grandparent, I take more time for my grandchildren. I'm doing more for my grandchildren than I did for my own children. But, still, I'm very, very good with my own children, too.

I've always thought that during that time from zero to six, what you see in that time is your luggage you'll take with you your whole life. Therefore, if the child is happy with that and it makes her happy, and she likes to take Miffy to bed, or Boris Bear or whatever, that's good, that gives warmth.

Edward M. Kennedy

Being a grandparent has renewed my energy and my sense of wonderment and curiosity. I see this wonderful innocence that's reflected in conversation: the goodness, the sweetness, the gentleness, and the sense of hope that children have.

The darker side of life people have to be educated to, but goodness springs from children. And if they're your grandchildren they're even closer to you. It's that sense of renewal that you get from being associated with them, or enjoying them, or spending time with them. I have wonderful grandchildren. One of them is Little Teddy. There's Little Teddy, Medium Teddy, and I'm Big Teddy. And Little Teddy loves Fenway Franks. Those are the frankfurters that they sell at Fenway Park in Boston, Massachusetts. And when we went last summer, I saw him eating Fenway Franks and he had the ketchup and the mustard and the relish on his nice clean shirt to show it. And I said, "How many Fenway Franks have you eaten, Teddy?" And he said (holds up five fingers), "Two, Grandpa, just two." And he went like this (folds three fingers down). So the honesty is there most of the time.

The interesting thing is that many of my children's friends became my friends and now my grandchildren's friends are also my friends.

We have family holidays and my friends, my family, my children's friends and my grand-children's friends come. We have twenty-five to thirty people in the house of every generation from age nought up to age eighty. And the interactions between the generations are very constructive. We prepare meals together and spend time together. I think that is great from everybody's point of view. Wonderful for the older generation and I think the younger generation enjoys it too.

As you get older you have less energy, and coping with children might be difficult. Coping with grand-children, whom you see frequently but not all the time, you can manage that all right. And I'm lucky. I have ten grandchildren and all of them have grown up near to me in Dublin and I have been very fortunate indeed in that. I get huge pleasure from them. The interesting thing is that many of my children's friends became my friends and now my grandchildren's friends are also my friends. Which is a very nice thing, to have people of that generation to be quite close to.

Vanessa Redgrave

It's the most wonderful thing to be a grandmother.

You sort of know why you're still on Earth round about that age when you come to be a grandmother. You sort of know why you're around, because grandmothers have a special biological place in nature.

Rosamunde Pilcher

You can have your grandchild for a day, and then you can give it back at the end of the day and you can go and pour yourself a drink.

A grandmother is not responsible for disciplining or teaching all the time. You can just enjoy it. You can have your grandchild for a day, and then you can give it back at the end of the day and you can go and pour yourself a drink. Which is lovely. I've got a very good relationship with all my grandchildren. I'm just very fond of them all and I have a different relationship with each one of them.

In marriage, an independence within each person is almost essential. I'm not one for a husband and wife doing everything together. It wouldn't have worked for us. My husband wasn't interested in anything I was interested in. He liked all his men friends and playing golf and doing things with his father, and luckily I wasn't a person who needed a lot of attention or company. It meant that I could go off and do my own thing. So my writing was good for the marriage. I'm awfully bad at talking about love, because there are so many different sorts of love. Obviously, it turns into a friendship, and it turns into a habit, and it turns into a way of life. But we were never a couple who people would say were made for each other, because we didn't share any of the same interests; but we were both independent and were ready to let the other one be independent and perhaps that's more important than that awful overworked word of "love." Space—isn't that the word people say nowadays? Let everybody have their own space. That's awfully important.

It's good for the children if you have an occupation that isn't just ironing and washing and cooking—which I've done all my life, I'm not decrying it—but you're a more interesting person to your children if you bring interesting people home, you go away and meet interesting people, you come back and tell people about it. It's a whole new side to a child's upbringing.

Kris Kristofferson

My experience with my eight children is very much the same as with my six grandchildren; the best part of it all is that they all love each other. I think I could just step out of the picture and they'd be fine.

I'm not quite the same as everybody else. Most people seem to think that being a grandparent, as opposed to being a parent, is the better experience because you have more of just the pure pleasure and less of the responsibility. With me, I guess I haven't had that much of the responsibility with either one; I have nothing but the love and affection of them. My experience with my eight children is very much the same as with my six grandchildren; the best part of it all is that they all love each other. I think I could just step out of the picture and they'd be fine.

The experience of working with The Highwaymen, with Johnny Cash and Willie Nelson and Waylon Jennings, was wonderful for me because these people were my heroes before I came to town, before I got successful as a songwriter. To be close friends with them…they were the best, the funniest, most creative people I'd ever been around. And to be able to work with them, to share the respect and affection that we had for each other, was one of the best things in my life. One of the best parts of my experience has been that people like Muhammad Ali, who I admired and respected, have turned out to be close friends—Johnny Cash, Roger Miller, Bob Dylan. Unfortunately, a lot of them are gone and it's only going to get worse as I get older, or as I don't. I feel really blessed to have been close to as many people that I respect.

The heart is what matters most of all. The act of compassion, of being able to put yourself in some-body else's shoes and to avoid any kind of harm to any other human being would be the best thing that could happen in the world. That's what is hopeful about Obama. I have a feeling that the United States could be a leader in improving things in the world, rather than what we are right now, the biggest problem in the world.

Yoko Ono

Be yourself, love yourself, and give that love to the world.

Be yourself and know that you count. And think about peace. Igniting peace is as simple as breathing. When you're imagining peace, you do understand that you can't kill somebody or you can't abuse somebody. You just imagine peace. You're in this trance. A beautiful trance of peace, of peaceness. That's what we're doing, all of us. We're trying to do that. We are each one of us an oasis for the world, and we have to realize that that's all we need to do. If you realize it, then it immediately happens. If we said, "I am dry, I'm just a desert," you immediately become a desert. You become what you want to become, what you think you want to be, what you think you are. It's very important. All of us have a super-god within us. You think about God: God is dead, God is in the church, God is wherever. No, God is in you. All you have to do is recognize that. A very simple example is a mother who is trying to save her child, who has this enormous power to move something that usually she couldn't move. We all have that power. Most people say, "That's so simplistic. Now she's getting so simple about her message. Is that because of her age?" And I think, "Wait a second, I've been studying minimalism since I was eighteen." The most important things in life are simple, like your breathing. And nobody's going to breathe dissonant sounds. You just breathe. Simple as that.

If anybody's thinking anything, it's going to affect us right away, and so all you have to do is just think about something positive, and it's going to affect the world. I have to tell you this funny story. I was in a car with a friend, and I suddenly started to want to eat a hamburger, and I don't eat meat. So I was thinking, "Why am I interested in eating a hamburger?" So I said, "I want a hamburger," and he said, "Oh really?" He just gave me a dirty look. And, later, I found out that he was so madly in love with hamburgers that even when he goes to Paris, he orders a special hamburger. And that was sort of affecting me. It's just a silly story in a way, but we're all affected by each other.

Your oasis and my oasis are communicating. Water is very interesting. We are, what is it, ninety percent water? Inside, we have that beautiful, clean water. The water can become dirty, too, from our thoughts. So we have to keep cleaning the water with our good thoughts, for when my water and your water are responding to each other. You're water, I'm water. So there's nothing that we can hide from each other. While we're trying to hide from each other, our water's already communicating. It's so beautiful. That's why when we say, we are all one, yes, we *are* all one. We are containers of water. When we're fighting, our heartbeats are in unison. Can you imagine that? When we're trying to kill each other, the heartbeat's going boom, boom, boom, together.

It's very important that now we start to think about our soul, our spirit. And when I say "soul" it has nothing to do with religions. Just our soul. We have a soul and a spirit. And we should start thinking about that instead of monetary gain. The common truth is that we are people and we should be proud of the fact that we're human beings. We should appreciate what we have. Our body's structure is incredible, how it works. It's like a miracle. Every day I think that we are a race of miracles. Be yourself, love yourself, and give that love to the world.

Graham Nash

A lot of the world's troubles stem from lack of self-image: not being confident in who you are and what you're supposed to be doing in life.

Wisdom could very well start with a little perspective. Let's understand a couple of basic things here. We're spinning around on a ball of mud that is one of billions and billions of balls of mud spinning through this universe, and the human life form is just one of perhaps many, many life forms throughout this universe. There's part of me that realizes that everything is completely meaningless, really. That if the last human being were to die in the next ten minutes, this Earth would still be spinning and it would rectify its growth pattern and human beings would be forgotten and the next life form would start, right? We need a little perspective about how unimportant what we do is. Having said that, I think it's very important to like yourself, it's important to love your family and love your friends and do things that help you grow and help you sleep. That's what I'm trying to do with my life.

When I was a child, all my friends also wanted to get into rock 'n' roll, because that's how you got the girls, right? They were being told, you know, they were being slapped on the head: "Get a real job," and, "This music's never going to last," and, "Go down to the mill where your dad used to work, and his grandfather," and, "If it was good enough for them, it's good enough for you." My mother and father never allowed me to go for that. It was an amazing thing: they were encouraging me. As a matter of fact, once I asked my mother just before she died why it was that my parents encouraged me to get into rock 'n' roll while everybody else's parents were dissuading them from that path. And

my mother said that it was once her ambition to be on the stage, which I'd never heard before. But I realized that, you know, during World War Two, which was when I was born, her ambitions were to keep the family alive during the bombing and the warfare and to keep them fed and try and educate them. But she wanted to be on the stage and she wanted to be a singer. And she wasn't about to allow circumstances to dictate my life. She didn't want anything dictating my life but me. It wasn't, "You've got to do what your dad did," and, "You've got to get a gold watch and work for a company for sixty years and then lie down and die while they get new blood in there." My mother and father never allowed me to fall for that and I'll always love them for that very small thing.

My father was a very simple man; we were quite poor. He bought a camera from a friend of his at work, and he would take me and my one sister to the zoo and take pictures of us, and I'd take a couple of pictures with his camera and then he'd set up a dark room. We only had four rooms in the entire house and they were very small, so he would take my bedroom and he'd put my blanket from the bed up against the window to block the light out, and he put a black piece of paper into a colourless liquid and waited and waited and waited, and then this image floated into view. My life has never been the same since that moment. That was a magic trick that I couldn't believe. Where did this image come from? Did little pieces of it fall from the sky onto the picture? How did this happen? That magic moment has never left me, to this moment. When I saw a particular image, which was a photograph taken by Diane Arbus of a boy in Central Park with a hand grenade, it was the first photograph I ever was moved to buy. And the reason I bought it was that it was showing me something about myself and my fellow human beings that I was aware of, but not deeply aware of, that there's an insanity that lives in all of us that can be triggered or can be not triggered. We all have the propensity for incredible violence and incredible love all at the same time. It's one of the human conditions that puzzles me greatly. So I've always wanted to see an image, want it enough to buy it, and then hang it in my house and look at it every time I walk down the hallway and have my kids look at it. Then I would change them to more ridiculous images and I would constantly revolve the images that I had, whether it be photographers, or Escher, or German Expressionist woodblocks, or anything that I thought would keep their mind moving. That's why I collect and that's why I show.

There's no booklet when it comes to parenting. You can't face a situation and go, "Oh, page forty-three, that's what I do." You can only raise kids, as my wife Susan and I did, as openly and as honestly as possible. We don't always get there, but we've always tried to be as honest as possible with our kids from the very start, from them being born—not talking to them in baby talk, no "goo goo goo dadda," it was always multi-syllable words and straight talk right from the word go. I would always

put images in my house that would make them question reality. I have a pretty absurd taste in images and I wanted to always stretch my kids' minds and not let them be ordinary, or feel that they couldn't do anything. I'm so proud of them. I'm sixty-six years old, my oldest son is thirty now, my second son is twenty-eight and my daughter is twenty-six. Where did that time go? And how did I bring up three incredibly secure—now this is how I feel, how they feel inside I don't know, but they look to me very secure—very compassionate, very interested in what other people are doing, very open, very funny, very self-confident. I'm very proud of my kids. How I got here, I don't know. I always took it a day at a time and we faced each problem with our hearts and our brains, and Susan and I have managed to bring three incredible children into this world.

I went out with Joni one morning, we had breakfast and she bought this vase that she liked in an antique store, and she brought it home and I lit the fire and she put flowers in the vase. A totally, completely normal situation. But I felt like I needed to go to the piano and say something about this ordinary moment with me and Joni, and the result was "Our House." I felt "Our House" coming through me. Normally I feel my songs coming from my insides, from whatever it is in there, a combination of my heart and my brain. Normally I feel it coming from me, but in that particular instance of "Our House" I felt it coming through me, and it was a different feeling, very different.

Dave Brubeck

If you don't love music, almost next to family, if you don't love it enough to want it regardless of what it does to you, don't get into it. Because it's going to demand much of you and of your family. If by doing music you have a great feeling of joy, and you'll accept all the hardship and your family accepts it, if it's the drive in your life and the beauty of expression in your life, then do it and know that it's going to be very difficult, but the love will make up for all the hardship.

Ravi Shankar

Marriage, musically, of course, is melody and rhythm.

But it's best when you marry someone half your age at the age of sixty-nine. No, seriously, love is the most important thing. And after the passion becomes much less, it is understanding, tolerance, and patience. These are the things that can maintain the marriage.

Music comes both from me and through me. We learn technique from our guru—all the fixed things—in the beginning. Then, for years, after working the dexterity and all the nuances, we feel the music. It all comes out; it just flows out. Music is an addiction. It is just like the ecstasy of finding gems in the vast ocean. It's sheer pleasure.

My husband was born under the sign of Cancer and I'm Sagittarius; he said, "We're both holding on, straining in opposite directions, you towards the light and me towards the dark." And in actual fact it was good because of that. The key to a good relationship is absolutely, undoubtedly: don't take the person for granted.

Always make the effort; and, hopefully

don't make the effort recognizably.

Don't ever think that they're going to come back to you just because you happen to be married.

Nadine Gordimer

What makes a marriage work? The mysterious thing of falling in love with somebody. It's the most wonderful thing.

And, of course, compatibility. By that I mean sharing. I'm not talking about whether you like going skiing or playing golf or going to the movies. That's very nice, but I'm talking particularly about your political opinions. I can't imagine in South Africa that I could have lived with, or even had a love affair with, somebody who was racist, who believed that apartheid was right. So I think to share this, to share such convictions about human freedom and about the decent way to treat people, this is, to me, the basis of a marriage. Because you will extend this to how you act towards your children, how you act towards your friends and, of course, how you act towards one another.

Chuck Close

A person's face is a kind of road map of the life that they've led.

Damned if I know what makes a marriage work. I have been married for forty years, and it's not one marriage: by then you've had four or five totally different marriages. You hope that you evolve in similar ways, in compatible ways, and that you now have a new reason to be with somebody. But they're going to be different from the previous reasons to be with them.

Jacques Pépin

Cooking is truly an act of love.

Cook with love. Sit down around the table and share food with your children and your family. It is very, very important. When my daughter Claudine was small, she'd get home, she was four years old, she'd say, "Mom, what's for dinner?" My wife would say, "Food," and that's where it stayed. We have been married forty-three years now, and I don't remember any time that we did not sit around the table, an hour every night, have an aperitif, open a bottle of wine, sometimes two. Claudine was there after school, and it's not necessarily a pleasant conversation to recap the day, but it's necessary, otherwise there is no communication.

You always communicate through cooking. You cannot cook indifferently, otherwise the food won't come across the right way. There is a great deal of love which goes into the making of food, and you always cook for the other; maybe the purest expression of love is to cook for someone. I don't see myself alone, standing in front of the top of the sink and making a soufflé of lobster. But as soon as someone else comes, whether it's your mother or your lover or your child or a friend, then you set up the table around you, you add to the table, and you open the wine.

Children never lie. I have a granddaughter and if she likes it, she says, "Papa, it's good," or, "It's no good." There is no sarcasm attached with this. I remember my daughter, when she was small, she was standing in her crib the first time that I gave her caviar and I put it on bread—butter and caviar—she licked it up and she said, "Encore, Papa."

You are more remote as a grandparent in some ways, so it's a freer situation: you can get the kid and when the kid starts smelling or gurgling or crying you can give it back to the parents. It's quite a different situation and it is a more casual and more tranquil type of relationship.

Madeleine Albright

Being a parent is one of the most difficult and demanding and rewarding things that you can possibly be.

You really are responsible for the day-to-day up-bringing of your child and you have to do some sanctions and try to figure out when to reward. With grandkids, you can just reward; and it is a purely beautiful and pleasant relationship, and you don't expect as much as you do from your children. It's just a perfect relationship.

Michael Parkinson

Mary, my wife, is much brighter than I am. And she saw me doing some silly things. She'd just stand back and say, "Well, he'll come back eventually."

A grandparent's role is to be all the things that parents can't be. To be that patient, wise, solid person, who unconditionally and without fail loves them.

You have to understand that your life does change. There is a strain put on family, but eventually it will all come right in the end. So we've just been very, very lucky. (It does help if you have a partner who loves you.) We have eight grandchildren now and I'm in a very, very happy stage of my life. I could bore you with complacency. I'm reliving those times that I didn't have time for with my children. When my kids were growing up, I was away. I was all over the world. I didn't see them for about two or three years, basically. I didn't realize how much I missed out until I had grandchildren. A grandparent's role is to be all the things that parents can't be. To be that patient, wise, solid person, who unconditionally and without fail loves them. You're that bastion. I see the love that my grandchildren have for my wife, particularly, and the effect that she has on their education and the way they look at things. We take them to the theater, we do the things parents don't have time to do. I take my granddaughters—I've got five of them—I take them to good restaurants and I say, "This is a good restaurant. Now, if you have a boyfriend who doesn't bring you here, don't go out with him. You tell him. You've got to go to the Ivy. Tell him you want tea at the Ritz. I mean, don't muck around." Grandparents can do that, you see. You can affect their life. You can make them dream.

Bill Withers

My grandmother always let me know that it was okay to be me.

There's a tendency to build a mold and then expect a kid to go fit himself in it. But people have different abilities and different tolerances. My grandmother was the biggest influence on me, insofar as my opinion of myself. When everybody said, "Billy stutters and he's never gonna grow," my grandmother would say, "Billy's cool. Maybe he's got something that you guys don't see." My grandmother always let me know that it was okay to be me, and that I might have something about me that may be a little bit different, that if I figured it out, I could apply it in some way to be okay.

Burt Bacharach

I want to hang in there as long as I can hang in. I want to stay as healthy as I can for as long as I can, just because I don't want to leave. I still feel I have work to do, music to write. If it all stopped now, I'd know I've done well and I should be proud of what I've done. But I want to hang in. I've got two young kids, a fifteen-year-old and a twelve-year-old, and a twenty-two-year-old son. I want to spend time with them. I had a daughter who tragically committed suicide last year, who tragically had such terrible, terrible problems with autism. Her Asperger's syndrome was very tough. I can say I wish I'd gotten to know her more or better, but it's very tough to communicate with someone that has it. And so I've got these three kids—you've got the time now, you are not so driven by your career, you are not so driven with, "I've got to get the next record out." Just enjoy it. I love these kids. They are special, great kids and I want to spend time with them.

Kurt Masur

I'm still a dreamer.

I thought about my childhood not so much as an education, but as a kind of getting examples from other people, from my mother. I was very close with my mother and I still feel she's there. Normally, if you have a connection with your mother, then all over the world you have the same kind of love. No religion can help you to be more clear about yourself than what your mother would say about what you just did and where you just failed. She always made me think about why…why am I such a dreamer? I'm still a dreamer. I felt, at first, helpless, weak, and soft. And then I started to experience that some of my dreams came true. And some of my expectations in life came true, without me doing anything about it.

When I started as a young conductor, people liked me because I was very friendly. Then, I remember, one of the orchestra musicians who later became my very good friend, came to me and said, "Dear friend, as a conductor, you behave very badly. If we are not playing good enough, you cannot smile. You're always happy. What's the matter?" Then I learned, step-by-step, what musicians expect from a conductor. They expect honesty. In the arts, you cannot lie. You cannot do a kind of diplomatic thing. If I speak to a musician in the orchestra, he should feel that I respect him highly. Otherwise, he wouldn't be willing to follow me. He must feel like a partner.

Buzz Aldrin

I feel very honored to have been in the right place at the right time, and to have lived up to the expectations I think other people have had of me. To deal with shortcomings, to learn how to appropriately look for help, to help other people as they are helping you—it all works out in a very smooth way, where we're not antagonizing other people. I try to be of service as much as I can. I feel that there is an obligation. I'm very proud of my country and I'm proud to be able to serve it. I'm not trying to be all things to all people. Wherever my talents are, I will use them to the most for the benefit of the future as I see it.

Bryce Courtenay

I traveled as a creative director for some large American agencies and suddenly realized that I was going all over the world, but was spending four days in a boardroom and catching a plane— I saw absolutely nothing. So I made a criteria as a fairly young advertising man that whenever I traveled I would, at the end of whatever I had to do, take two days at the end of it, regardless, for myself, and have a look around. By the end of fifty years I had a book with addresses of everybody I'd met who I liked, for fifty years. Every day I would write, starting from A going to Z, two postcards to two people in the book; and occasionally I'd get a letter back. I was communicating with these people I'd met all my life. Travel, for me, is people. Now, may I tell you a lovely story? In 1956, I'm in Kathmandu and I have to go to an advertising event in Pakistan. I shared a room with a Pakistani guy and all he wanted to do was have a good time. He was wasting his time. He's supposed to be at London Polytechnic or something, and I was going through university. He offered to share his room with me and it was cheap and I could do that. Suddenly, I'm in Karachi, thirty-seven years later. I'd written him a card saying, "Hey, look, I'm coming to Karachi if you're there."

I've sent him a card every year, but haven't heard from him. I arrive in Pakistan, and the human donkeys are on the plane—they carry these huge loads and then they come off the plane for merchants and they drop their merchandise. They put me right at the back, and the hostess says, "Would you mind letting the human donkeys get off first?" Forgive that expression, but that's what she actually said. I said, "Of course not." God, I felt sorry for them; it was just tough stuff. Eventually the plane is empty and I'm still sitting there and I said, "Can I go now?" And she said "No, no, no, not yet." What's happening here? And finally she says, "Come." I walk out and there is a battalion piping me down and a general, who's my mate, welcoming me to Pakistan. They drive me in a convoy to the Governor's house and that's where I stayed. He's general of the army. General Khan. That's what travel means. Travel means people: friends, touching, sensing. It's not about just seeing. It's the experience of life. And the one thing you do understand about it is that in the ordinary world, generosity overpowers greed. People are, by their natures, wonderfully generous. And that comes back to that wisdom thing we talked about earlier: be nice, be kind, be

joyous, because everybody else will be. They recognize it. That is the original wisdom. That's the world's wisdom, not mine. That's what the world teaches you: that humans have an infinite capacity to be generous. They may be evil, they may be awful in so many respects, but that's always men. Individuals can be evil and the world has got lots of bad men (and some bad women, but mostly men). But, generally speaking, people are generous and kind.

There is no fear. There is only consequence. I've been mugged several times. Once, in New York, after I picked myself up, I said to the guy, "What's the matter?" He said, "Give me your wallet, buddy." And I said, "No." He thumped me again. So I got up, and said, "Hey, what's the problem?" And he said, "My family hasn't eaten for three days." I said, "I've got lots of money. Here, we're going to Woolworths." We went in and I bought them a thousand bucks worth of groceries. That guy went into the address book. Now, I have one sad story to tell. I was mugged in South Africa as I stepped out of the airport four years ago and everything went—my luggage was smashed, everything. The book went. The saddest thing in my life. I lost all my addresses. I had every radio station in South Africa saying, "Look, keep the cheques, keep the money, keep everything. Just return the book."

Be nice, be kind, be joyous, because everybody else will be.

Biographies

Madeleine Albright
15 May 1937
Prague
Czech Republic

Madeleine Albright's family fled Nazi persecution in 1939, first to England and then to the USA, where she earned several degrees in international affairs, including a Ph.D. Albright worked on the Muskie presidential campaign in 1972, and later became a staff member of both the National Security Council and the White House. During the Republican administrations of the 1980s and early 1990s she lectured in international affairs at Georgetown University. In 1992, President Clinton appointed her UN Ambassador and five years later she became the first female US Secretary of State (1997–2001). She is a co-founder of the Center for National Policy.

Buzz Aldrin
20 January 1930
Montclair, New Jersey
USA

Buzz Aldrin graduated from West Point Military Academy and served in Korea and Germany as a jet fighter pilot. He received his doctorate in astronautics from the Massachusetts Institute of Technology, and was chosen by NASA to join the astronaut corps in 1963. Buzz and Neil Armstrong became the first two men to set foot on the moon on 20 July 1969 during the Apollo 11 mission. Upon his return, Aldrin received many awards from countries worldwide, including the US Presidential Medal of Freedom. He has authored six books, with the seventh to be published in 2009. He travels and lectures throughout the world (with his wife of twenty years, Lois Driggs Aldrin, a Stanford alumna) sharing his latest ideas for exploring the universe.

Alan Arkin
26 March 1934
New York, New York
USA

Alan Arkin formed the folk group
The Tarriers after dropping out
of college, and co-wrote "The
Banana Boat Song," which would
later become a hit for Harry
Belafonte. His screen debut came
in 1957, followed by roles on and
off Broadway, and he won a
Tony Award in 1963 for *Enter
Laughing*. Arkin's role in *The
Russians Are Coming* earned him
the first of three Academy Award
nominations. In 2006 Arkin won
an Academy Award for his role
in the film *Little Miss Sunshine*.
He has written numerous songs,
as well as science fiction and
children's books.

Burt Bacharach
12 May 1928
Kansas City, Missouri
USA

Burt Bacharach studied music
at McGill University, the Mannes
School of Music, and the Music
Academy of the West. He spent
two years in the army playing
piano before teaming up with
lyricist Hal David in 1957. The pair
wrote twenty-two Top 40 hits for
Dionne Warwick, including "Do
You Know the Way to San Jose?",
as well as songs for many other
performers. Bacharach's fifty-year
run on the charts includes
seventy Top 40 hits in the USA,
fifty-two Top 40 hits in the UK,
over five hundred compositions,
three Academy Awards (two for
"Raindrops Keep Falling on My
Head" and one for "Arthur's
Theme"), and six Grammy
Awards.

Dave Brubeck
6 December 1920
Concord, California
USA

Dave Brubeck studied music at
the University of the Pacific. He
graduated in 1942 before serving
in the US Army. After World War
Two he continued his studies
at Mills College under Darius
Milhaud, who encouraged him to
play jazz. In 1951, he formed the
Dave Brubeck Quartet and
released albums such as *Jazz
Goes to College*. Brubeck's music
is notable for unusual time
signatures and his 1959 album
Time Out included "Take Five"
set in 5/4 time, which has become
a jazz standard. He received a
Grammy Lifetime Achievement
Award in 1996.

Dick Bruna
23 August 1927
Utrecht
The Netherlands

Dick Bruna, who has written and illustrated over one hundred children's books, began his career as a graphic artist, and in 1955 wrote *Nijntje* (*Miffy,* in English) which has been translated into forty languages and made into a television series. Sales from his books exceed eighty million copies worldwide, and he regularly makes his illustrations available in support of UNICEF and other humanitarian organizations. Bruna was knighted in 1993 by Queen Beatrix and made a Companion of the Order of Oranje-Nassau.

Chuck Close
5 July 1940
Monroe, Washington
USA

Chuck Close studied art at the University of Washington and Yale University before winning a Fulbright scholarship to Vienna. His first solo exhibition in 1970 demonstrated his photorealism technique of breaking photographs into a grid and enlarging the contents of each square by hand, an approach for which he was to become well-known through his massive-scale portraits. In 1988, Close suffered a spinal blood clot that left him partially paralyzed and wheelchair-bound, but he continued to paint with a brush strapped onto his fingers. In 1998, New York's Museum of Modern Art mounted a major exhibition of his work.

Billy Connolly
24 November 1942
Glasgow
Scotland

Billy Connolly left school at the age of fifteen to become a shipyard welder before forming a folk-pop duo called The Humblebums, who recorded three albums. His first solo album, *Billy Connolly Live!*, released in 1972, featured Connolly as a singer-songwriter and musician but it wasn't until he appeared on BBC's *Parkinson* in 1975 that he became a household name as a comedian. In 2003, he was awarded a CBE (Commander of the British Empire) and a BAFTA Lifetime Achievement Award.

Bryce Courtenay
14 August 1933
Johannesburg, Gauteng
South Africa

A naturalized Australian, Bryce Courtenay's early years, before boarding school, were spent in a village in the Lebombo Mountains of South Africa. He later won a British university scholarship but was banned from returning to South Africa as a result of "politically unacceptable activity." Courtenay emigrated to Australia in the late 1950s and worked in advertising before taking up writing at the age of fifty-five. His first book, *The Power of One,* became an enduring bestseller. He has subsequently written over twenty books and remains one of Australia's most successful authors.

Judi Dench
9 December 1934
York, North Yorkshire
England

Considered one of the greatest actors of post-war Britain, Judi Dench trained at the Central School of Speech and Drama. In 1958, she made her Broadway debut in *Twelfth Night* and three years later she helped form the Royal Shakespeare Company. She broke into film in 1964, winning a BAFTA four years later for the TV series *Talking to a Stranger.* Her many awards include six Laurence Olivier Awards, a Tony, two Golden Globes, an Academy Award, and nine BAFTA awards. In 1988, she was awarded a DBE (Dame Commander of the British Empire) and, in 2005, a CHDBE (Companion of Honour).

Garret FitzGerald
9 February 1926
Dublin
Ireland

Garret FitzGerald was one of the Republic of Ireland's most popular politicians and was its Taoiseach (prime minister) twice, from July 1981 – February 1982 and again from December 1982 – March 1987. He obtained a BA and Ph.D. from University College Dublin and entered the Irish Senate in 1965 and the House of Representatives in 1969. In 1973, FitzGerald became Minister for Foreign Affairs and when his party, Fine Gael, was defeated in 1977 he became leader and led a minority coalition government in 1981. He resigned as party leader after the 1987 election defeat, and retired in 1992.

Nadine Gordimer
20 November 1923
Springs, Gauteng
South Africa

Nadine Gordimer published her first short story at the age of fifteen and went on to complete fourteen novels, nineteen short-story collections, several works of non-fiction, and a number of television scripts based on her works. Her writings center on the effects of apartheid, of which she was a passionate opponent, and have been translated into forty languages even though many of them were banned in South Africa. In 1974, Gordimer won the Booker Prize for Fiction for *The Conservationist*. She was awarded the Nobel Prize for Literature in 1991, and in 2007 became a Knight of the National Order of the Legion of Honour (France).

Denis Healey
30 August 1917
Mottingham, Kent
England

Denis Healey grew up in Yorkshire. Educated at the University of Oxford, he was for two years a member of the Communist Party, but joined the Labour Party after World War Two. He served as a Member of Parliament for Leeds South West for forty years from 1952, and was Her Majesty's Secretary of State for Defence from 1964–1970, and Chancellor of the Exchequer from 1974–1979. In 1992, he entered the House of Lords when he was awarded a life peerage.

Edward M. Kennedy
22 February 1932
Boston, Massachusetts
USA

The youngest of eight siblings, including former President John F. Kennedy and Senator Robert F. Kennedy, Edward M. Kennedy was educated at Harvard University, the International Law School (The Hague), and University of Virginia Law School. In 1962, he was elected senator for Massachusetts and is currently the second-longest-serving senator in the USA. He is a prominent advocate for social policies such as national health insurance, consumer protection, and social welfare.

Kris Kristofferson
22 June 1936
Brownsville, Texas
USA

Kris Kristofferson won a Rhodes scholarship to the University of Oxford, and then served in the US Army as a helicopter pilot, eventually resigning to take up country music in Nashville. His compositions have been performed by over four hundred and fifty artists and he has recorded twenty-four albums. In 1971, he won a Grammy for "Help Me Make It Through the Night." He has also had a long screen career, with over one hundred film and television appearances including *A Star is Born* (1976), which earned him a Golden Globe for Best Actor. He was inducted into the Country Music Hall of Fame in 2004.

Nelson Mandela
18 July 1918
Mvezo, Eastern Cape
(formerly in the Transkei)
South Africa

Nelson Mandela qualified in law in 1942 and two years later joined the African National Congress (ANC). Anti-discrimination activities led to his arrest for treason in 1956, although he was acquitted in 1961 before being rearrested in 1962. While still incarcerated, he stood trial with other ANC leaders for plotting to overthrow the government and was sentenced to life imprisonment, a term he served mainly on Robben Island. His reputation grew during his twenty-seven-year-long imprisonment, and after his release in 1990 he worked tirelessly to create a new multi-racial South Africa. In 1993 he shared the Nobel Peace Prize with F.W. de Klerk, and the following year became South Africa's first democratically elected President (1994–1999).

Kurt Masur
18 July 1927
Brieg, Silesia
Poland
(formerly in Germany)

Conductor Kurt Masur studied piano and cello in Breslau, and then moved to the Leipzig Conservatory to study piano, conducting, and composition. Masur has directed orchestras around the world, notably the New York Philharmonic, the Orchestre National de France, the Leipzig Gewandhaus Orchestra, the London Philharmonic and the Israel Philharmonic. He has made more than one hundred recordings and received numerous honors including the Cross with Star of the Order of Merits (Germany, 1995), the Gold Medal of Honor for Music (National Arts Club, USA, 1996), Commander of the National Order of the Legion of Honour (France, 1997), and the Commander Cross of Merit (Poland, 1999).

Jeanne Moreau
23 January 1928
Paris, Île-de-France
France

Jeanne Moreau trained at the
Conservatoire in Paris. At the age
of nineteen, she made her
theatrical debut at the Avignon
Festival. By the late 1950s,
Moreau had transitioned into film
and was directed by some of the
period's best-known avant-garde
directors. Her biggest success
came under Francois Truffaut's
direction in the film *Jules et Jim*
in 1962. In 1988, the American
Academy of Motion Pictures
presented a life tribute to Moreau.
In her career she has also worked
behind the scenes as a writer,
producer, and director.

Graham Nash
2 February 1942
Blackpool, Lancashire
England

Musician and photographer
Graham Nash co-founded The
Hollies in 1961, one of the UK´s
most successful groups whose
hits included "On a Carousel." In
1968, he moved to the USA and
formed Crosby, Stills & Nash,
whose first release was the hit
"Marrakesh Express," written by
Nash. In 1969, they performed at
Woodstock, the same year their
first album won a Grammy Award.
In 1990, he co-founded Nash
Editions, a digital printmaking
company, which was recognized
in 2005 by the Smithsonian
Institution for its role in the
invention of digital fine art printing.

Rupert Neudeck
14 May 1939
Gdańsk, Pomorskie
(formerly Free City of Danzig)
Poland

Neudeck lived in Danzig until his
family had to flee the city after
World War Two, when it came
under Polish rule. He attended
college in West Germany, and
later worked as a correspondent
for a German radio station. In
1978 he founded Cap Anamur, an
organization focused on helping
refugees from countries in turmoil.
More recently, Neudeck founded
Gruenhelme (Green Helmets),
which reconstructs villages in
destroyed regions.

Nick Nolte
8 February 1941
Omaha, Nebraska
USA

Nick Nolte attended Arizona
State University on a football
scholarship but dropped out to
become an actor at the Pasadena
Playhouse. He studied at Stella
Adler Academy in Los Angeles
and traveled for several years,
performing in regional theaters.
A breakthrough role in the 1976
television series *Rich Man, Poor
Man* earned Nolte an Emmy
Award nomination, and since then
he has played a wide variety of
characters in more than fifty films,
earning two Academy Award
nominations and winning a
Golden Globe, as well as a New
York Film Critics Circle Award for
Best Actor.

Yoko Ono
18 February1933
Tokyo, Kanto
Japan

Yoko Ono moved to New York at
the age of eighteen and gained
notoriety when she opened the
Chambers Street Series in her
loft, where she presented some
of her earliest conceptual and
performance artwork. In 1966,
Ono met John Lennon and they
started their highly publicized
relationship. Ono continues
to create performance and
abstract pieces. Her recent work,
Sky Ladders, was unveiled at
the 2008 Liverpool Biennial.

Michael Parkinson
28 March 1935
Cudworth, South Yorkshire
England

Michael Parkinson has interviewed
over two thousand people on his
eponymous show. He began his
career as a journalist before
moving into television current
affairs. In 1971, he began hosting
Parkinson, which ran until 2007,
interviewing guests as diverse as
Muhammad Ali and Miss Piggy. He
was awarded a CBE (Commander
of the British Empire) for services
to broadcasting in 2000, and in
2008 was made a Knight Bachelor.

Jacques Pépin
18 December 1935
Bourg-en-Bresse, Ain
France

One of America's best-known
chefs, Pépin trained in Paris at the
Plaza Athénée. He was chef to
three French heads of state,
including Charles de Gaulle,
before moving to the USA in
1959, where he studied French
literature at Columbia University.
He has published twenty-five
cookbooks and hosted nine
television cooking series, and his
most famous book, *La Technique,*
is considered a seminal text on
the principles of French cuisine. In
2004, Pépin became a Knight of
the National Order of the Legion
of Honour (France).

Rosamunde Pilcher
22 September 1924
Lelant, Cornwall
England

Internationally best-selling author
Rosamunde Pilcher served in the
Women's Royal Naval Service
during World War Two, and the
first of ten novels, written under
the pseudonym Jane Fraser, was
published in 1951. Four years
later, Pilcher began writing under
her own name and international
fame came in 1987 when *The
Shell Seekers* topped the *New
York Times* bestseller list. Several
of her novels have been made
into films and television series. In
2002, she was awarded an OBE
(Order of the British Empire).

Vanessa Redgrave
30 January 1937
London
England

Vanessa Redgrave trained at the
Central School of Speech and
Drama. She joined the Royal
Shakespeare Company in the
1960s, by which time she had
already made her film debut and
appeared on stage in the West
End. She is the recipient of
numerous awards, including two
Golden Globes and an Academy
Award, and in 1967 was awarded
a CBE (Commander of the British
Empire). Redgrave has supported
a number of humanitarian causes
since the 1960s and now serves as
a UNICEF Goodwill Ambassador.

Ravi Shankar
7 April 1920
Varanasi, Uttar Pradesh
India

Desmond Tutu
7 October 1931
Klerksdorp, Transvaal
South Africa

Massimo Vignelli, Lella Vignelli
Massimo 10 January 1931
Milan, Lombardia
Lella 13 August 1934
Udine, Friuli-Venezia Giulia
Italy

Ravi Shankar is one of the leading Indian musicians of the modern era. A legend in India and abroad, Shankar has melded Indian music into Western forms: he has written concertos, ballets, and film scores. In the 1960s, Shankar attracted worldwide attention for appearing at the Monterey Pop Festival and Woodstock, and for teaching Beatle George Harrison to play the sitar. His film score for *Gandhi* earned him nominations for both Academy and Grammy awards, and he has received twelve honorary doctorates as well as the Bharat Ratna, India's highest civilian honor. In 1986, he became a member of the Rajya Sabha, India's Upper House of Parliament.

Desmond Mpilo Tutu, Archbishop Emeritus, began his career as a teacher before studying theology, and was ordained as an Anglican priest in 1960. In 1975, he became the first black Dean of St Mary's Cathedral in Johannesburg, followed by appointments as the Bishop of Lesotho, General Secretary of the South African Council of Churches, Anglican Archbishop of Cape Town and Primate of the Church of the Province of South Africa. He gained international fame as an anti-apartheid activist in the 1980s and was awarded the Nobel Peace Prize in 1984 and the Gandhi Peace Prize in 2007.

Massimo and Lella Vignelli met in Venice while studying architecture. They established the Vignelli Office of Design and Architecture in Milan in 1960, moved to New York in 1966, and founded Vignelli Associates in 1971. They have worked with numerous high-profile companies including IBM, American Airlines, and New York's Metropolitan Transportation Authority, for whom they designed the iconic signage for the New York City subway system. The Vignellis have received multiple awards including the AIGA Gold Medal, and the National Lifetime Achievement Award from the Cooper-Hewitt, National Design Museum in New York. They were inducted into the Interior Design Hall of Fame in 1988.

Bill Withers
4 July 1938
Slab Fork, West Virginia
USA

After a childhood in the coal
mining towns of West Virginia,
Withers joined the navy at the
age of seventeen and in 1967
moved to Los Angeles to pursue
a music career. The single "Ain't
No Sunshine," from his debut
album, became an international
hit, earning him the first of nine
Grammy nominations. Withers's
songs have been recorded by
artists from almost every genre,
and he has received numerous
awards, including three Grammy
Awards. He was inducted into the
Songwriters Hall of Fame in 2005.

Andrew Wyeth
12 July 1917 – 16 January 2009
Chadds Ford, Pennsylvania
USA

Andrew Wyeth started drawing
as a young child and was taught
art formally by his father, a well-
known illustrator. He worked
primarily in watercolors and egg
tempera, and his first one-man
show in Maine in 1937, of
watercolors painted around the
family's summer home at Port
Clyde, was the first of many
successes. Wyeth was
considered one of the world's
most collectable living artists,
and, in 1970, became the first
artist to hold a one-man exhibition
at the White House. He was
awarded the Congressional
Medal of Honor (USA) in 1988.